IMAGES
of America

MACOMB TOWNSHIP

Shown is a survey map of Macomb Township from 1859. (Courtesy of the Mike Ellis collection.)

On the Cover: Hall Road (Michigan Highway 59) and Tilch Road are seen here in 1920. Today there is an eight-lane divided highway in Hall Road's place. (Courtesy of the Milt Miller collection.)

IMAGES
of America

MACOMB TOWNSHIP

Linda Osborne Cynowa

ARCADIA
PUBLISHING

ISBN 978-1-4671-0557-6

Published by Arcadia Publishing
Charleston, South Carolina

Printed in the United States of America

Library of Congress Control Number: 2020934424

For all general information, please contact Arcadia Publishing:
Telephone 843-853-2070
Fax 843-853-0044
E-mail sales@arcadiapublishing.com
For customer service and orders:
Toll-Free 1-888-313-2665

Visit us on the Internet at www.arcadiapublishing.com

This book is dedicated to all the historians and archivists who work very hard to keep the pieces of our past safe for future generations.

"I've always felt that a person's intelligence is directly reflected by the number of conflicting points of view he can entertain simultaneously on the same topic."

—Abigail Adams

Contents

Acknowledgments

It is with the greatest appreciation that I thank Julie Oparka, certified archivist at the Romeo District Library and Community Archives, for her continued support, unending help, and assistance in producing this project; Janet Dunn, Macomb township supervisor; Peggy Accardo, Dave Piper, Milt Miller, Wayne Oehmke, and Joseph Witulski of the Macomb Historical Commission; Theresa Mann at the Mount Clemens Public Library; Shelly Stier Henshaw, who was always there to answer what ever question would arise; Joy Raska Jennett for opening numerous doors and giving so freely of her time; Pastor Mike Lutz from Immanuel Lutheran Church; Janet Gozdor, Shelley Fowler, May Schramm, and Dawn Miller, historians for St. Peter Lutheran Church; historian Cynthia Donahue; Debbie Rak at St. Isidore Catholic Church; Karen Malburg Goodhue; Terry Gioke from the Friends of Ray Township Library; Larry and Christine Pretzer; John Eschenburg; Mike Ellis; Maryanne Deneweth; Jeff Altermatt; Andrew Andy Johnson; Pete Schoenherr; Bill Rang; Matt and Mike Giroux; Shirley Petitpren; Dana Deneweth; Cracklewood Golf Course; and Brittany Cynowa for her research abilities, historical interest, and always getting me back on to the right path again. The majority of the images used in this book are individually credited, and to all that I did not mention above, I give my heartfelt thanks for permission to use these images to help preserve this history of Macomb Township.

INTRODUCTION

In the beginning, there was only a vast wilderness; the Chippewas, the Delawares, the Objiwa, the Iroquois, and the Potawatomi became the first Michiganders and called this area home. Michigan became a separate territory in 1805, and by 1818, Gov. Lewis Cass made the area of Macomb the third county in the state.

The first entry of land in the town was made by G.B. and D.G. Ginochio, from Detroit, of the east half of the northeast quarter of section 35 on August 12, 1820. On June 26, 1821, Alfred Ashley of Mount Clemens purchased the east half of the southwest quarter of the same section from the government. It was long known that the Haskins mill was part of that section and evidence of shrewd foresight for Ashley. Over the years, the southeast corner of the township seemed to attract land purchasers or settlers, most probably because of its proximity to the then-thriving Mount Clemens, only nine miles away.

In 1830, John and David Crawford of Yates County, New York, purchased the northeast quarter of section 1, where the history of the Crawford Settlement began. In the same year, on November 13, Lester Giddings purchased the west half of the southwest quarter of section 5. Daniel Miller made a purchase of the east half of the northwest quarter of section 8 on May 10, 1831.

On March 17, 1834, the township of Macomb was organized by an act of the territorial legislature. It was at first composed of what are now the townships of Chesterfield and Macomb. In 1842, Macomb became territorially independent. The township was named for Alexander Macomb, who was a highly decorated veteran of the War of 1812.

Although many of the governmental land plots were purchased before the organization of the township, the land sales became very frequent immediately after it became independent. In 14 years from 1820 to 1834, about 5,000 of the over 23,000 acres passed into private ownership. The remaining 18,000 acres were sold in the next three years after the organization.

At a fairly early date, a large number of German immigrants settled in Macomb Township because of the rich soil and land. Macomb was largely part of the lumber and logging industry of southeastern Michigan in the late 19th century and early 20th century. Logs were transported south from Wolcott Mill in Ray Township down the middle branch of the Clinton River to sawmills. The route taken became known as Romeo Plank, the same name as the modern-day road used to travel the very same route.

Macomb Township had three unincorporated communities. Waldenburg is the name given to a settlement at the corners of sections 28, 29, 32, and 33, what is today the intersection of 21 Mile and Romeo Plank Roads. A general store, church and school, wagon shop, and other businesses were found there. As time went on, 22 Mile Road and Romeo Plank Road became more officially thought of as Waldenburg. The Macomb Post Office was moved to Waldenburg on March 29, 1860, and lasted until 1906. The building that Stier Hardware was in was originally located across the street from where it ended up and served as a dance hall for the community. It was moved in 1903. Next to the hardware store was the Waldenburg Tavern, still located in the same spot as the Waldenburg Bar today.

Macomb Corners, located in the northwest corner of the township, had a post office by 1830. A general store and a Methodist church and grade school were also located on this planked toll road, where the road and stagecoach lessened in importance with the coming of the railroad.

Meade was located in the northeast portion of the township, on the boundary with Ray Township at 26 Mile Road, also called Marine City Highway and North Avenue. Its first name was Crawford or Crawford Settlement; Vienna was chosen as the post office name in 1838, with Stewart Taylor as its first postmaster. The Crawford name came from a Revolutionary War veteran, but after the Civil War battle at Gettysburg, the village was renamed in honor of Gen. George Gordon Meade. The Crawford Settlement landowners built the second school in Macomb Township. This school was the first in the county to offer algebra during the 1846–1847 school year. Now the Meade Cemetery and a few street signs are all that is left of the village of Meade, which operated as a town until 1906.

By the 1920s–1930s, the forests provided the lumber needed to build the barns, homes, and plank roads, such as Romeo Plank Road. There were two sawmills, with one located on 21 Mile Road northwest of Romeo Plank Road and another northwest of 24 Mile and Romeo Plank Roads before relocating to the east corner of 25 Mile and Romeo Plank Roads. The large oak trees were cut with axes and two-man saws, but the stumps required a trip to Stier Hardware at 22 Mile and Romeo Plank Roads for the dynamite needed to finally clear the land. Some stands of trees were left untouched and can still be found on certain farms today.

Each year, the local farmers gathered together and helped one another with the harvesting of their field crops of hay and straw. After the conclusion of this work, families gathered and celebrated the good harvest with a community dinner that made the consumption of beer and whiskey an integral part of those days.

By the early 1970s, a good portion of the farming land was sold for the development of much-needed housing, because many families from other areas would come and find their future here. The life they wanted to raise their children would be best found here in Macomb Township.

One

Macomb Township Farming

Farmers are cleaning the ditches with board scrapers. They could also use the boards with horses to remove the dirt. Around 1920, Harold Miller (right) works with a number of other gentlemen on Hall Road (now mostly known as Michigan Highway 59), which runs alongside his farm, located off Hall Road and Tilch Road. (Courtesy of the Milt Miller collection.)

Felix Deneweth (1825–1911) was born in West Flanders, Belgium, and settled around 1856 in Macomb Township, where he purchased property and started a sawmill and gristmill on Hall Road between Card Road and North Avenue. His first wife, Amelia DeWulf (1826–1869), passed away, and he then married his second wife, Anna Richwine Deneweth (1842–1920). Below, the Deneweth home, built around 1920 on Hall Road, is one of three homes on the farm property where Felix's three sons—George, Frank, and Philip—lived and worked; it still stands today. (Both, courtesy of the Maryanne Deneweth collection.)

One of Felix's sons, George Richwine Deneweth (1879–1957), married Mary O'Brien Deneweth (1886–1971) after she emigrated from Canada to attend nursing school at St. Joseph's in Mount Clemens; she graduated in 1913. The couple is seen here around 1910. George and Mary went on to raise their son, George Richwine Deneweth Jr. (1921–1990), who grew up to become a Macomb County Circuit Court judge. (Both, courtesy of the Maryanne Deneweth collection.)

Felix Deneweth's sons, George, Frank, and Philip, started the dairy in 1913. By 1916, they expanded the farm to what it is today. Phillip was the carpenter, Frank raised chickens, and George raised cows. The image of the Deneweth Bros. Dairy wagon has Frank Deneweth proudly posing for the photographer. Below, a young James Shanahan visits his uncle Frank Deneweth's farm on Hall Road in 1910. (Above, courtesy of the Maryanne Deneweth collection; below, courtesy of the Andrew Andy Johnson collection.)

By 1875, Zacharias Flory (1826–1891) and Elizabeth Frede Flory (1833–1909) purchased an 80-acre property on Hall Road in section 34, between Heydenreich and Card Roads. They raised eight children on this farm—six boys and two girls. One of their sons, Conrad Flory (1866–1929), and his wife, Carolyn Falkenhagen Flory (1867–1946), took over the running of the same 80-acre produce farm after the death of his father and kept the farm in the family until at least 1925. One of Conrad and Carolyn's daughters, Emma, married John Eschenburg from the Eschenburg farm on 24 Mile Road. Below, Eschenburg is pictured while courting Emma. (Both, courtesy of the John Eschenburg collection.)

On July 1, 1919, Michigan Highway 59 was designated along a road between Michigan Highway 10 in Pontiac and Michigan Highway 19 in Mount Clemens. By 1932, Michigan Highway 59 was moved to follow Hall Road exclusively on the east end of Macomb. The Michigan Highway 59 freeway crosses the border between Sterling Heights and Shelby Township and ends at Van Dyke Avenue in Utica, where Michigan Highway 59 becomes a boulevard called Hall Road. This section of the road is considered the main street in Macomb County because, as time moved forward, it became home to a wide variety of shopping and dining areas. Early Hall Road is seen here around 1900, when it was still safe for youngsters to stand in the road. Below, it is seen around 1960, when a stronger bridge was needed where Hall Road crosses over the north branch of the Clinton River near Elizabeth Road, which is still under construction. (Both, courtesy of the Maryanne Deneweth collection.)

Horace Cady and his wife, Susan Conner Cady, were married in 1825, four years after Horace moved to Macomb Township. His occupation was that of a farmer, but he was supervisor of the township for 15 years, justice of the peace for one term, county treasurer for two years, and a member of the Michigan House of Representatives in 1865. Horace and Susan parented five children. Pictured here, son John Cleveland Cady (1831–1908) became a prominent farmer by furthering his father's work. In 1863, John married Mary Ellen Smith (1834–1912); they helped run the 100-acre farm on section 35 off of Hall Road south of North Avenue. (Both, courtesy of the Mount Clemens Public Library collection.)

Five generations of Webers lived in Macomb Township for over 100 years. August Weber settled this piece of property in the mid-1800s; they had moved from Germany and bought the land along the Middle Branch of the Clinton River. After August, son Albert and his wife, Amelia, raised five children in this home and became very involved in the construction of the new Immanuel Lutheran Church on the corner of 21 Mile and Romeo Plank Roads. Robert took over the farm after his father's passing. Robert married Helen Stade and raised three children on the farm at 19703 21 Mile Road. As the years passed and the property was sold, the township found it a perfect place for families and children and called it Waldenburg Park. (Courtesy of the Larry and Christine Pretzer collection.)

This is an aerial view of the Henry Rocker farm at 215 Shoemaker Road, now 21 Mile Road, across from the Burning Tree Golf Course. The farm was passed down through generations of the Rocker family and designated a Michigan Centennial Farm. The home was demolished, and the land was developed as a subdivision in the 1990s. (Courtesy of the Mount Clemens Public Library collection.)

This c. 1888 cabinet card portrait shows the Henry Rocker family. From left to right are (first row) Otto H. Rocker (1887–1966), Ariel Rocker (1884–1939), and Herman F. Rocker (1882–1945); (second row) Fredrika Wilhelmine Henrietta Schultz Rocker (1856–1922) and Heinrich "Henry" Rocker (1844–1923). (Courtesy of the Mount Clemens Public Library Local History collection.)

This early image of the Henry Rocker farmhouse shows Fredrika seated on the porch and Henry and his children, along with a faithful companion, posing for the photographer. (Courtesy of the Mount Clemens Public Library collection.)

This aerial view of the George and Theodore Beaufait home and farm on 21 Mile and Card Roads shows the barns and silo. Their original farm was in the area where Selfridge Air National Guard Base is now located. (Both, courtesy of the Mount Clemens Public Library collection.)

This building was erected in 1874, when Romeo Plank Road was just that—an old plank road. When other main roads got wet and muddy, this was one of the first stops to pay the toll needed to get through to Mount Clemens to further one's business. The building was also a post office, with a dry goods store in the front and a barber chair and a bar in the back. Water Kling purchased the building in the 1940s and called it Kling's Tavern. (Courtesy of the Claude and Josephine Giroux collection.)

By the 1970s, Goldie Michaels became the part-owner and operator of the building now called Goldies, where, at one point, the road commission lost some bright yellow paint that "fell off" the back of its truck and soon found itself as the new outside color of Goldies. By 1977, Claude and Josephine Giroux purchased the bar, and Goldies was then in new hands. To this day, Goldies continues to meet the needs of the community that surrounds it, with Claude and Josephine's sons Mike and Matt Giroux still running the business. (Courtesy of the Claude and Josephine Giroux collection.)

Francis Wiegand started farming in 1860 in Warren, Michigan. Francis's son Philip took half of the family homestead and planted orchard and vineyard crops on the land. Soon, pines and spruces were added, as well as, by 1934, perennial flowers. In 1941, Raymond Weigand married Alice LaGrou, and with the knowledge she gained from her family, she contributed to the continuing success of the business. Ray and Alice had 13 children—9 girls and 4 boys—who all played a major roll on the farm. (Both, courtesy of the Ray Wiegand's Nursery collection.)

As the city moved in around them in Warren, the family purchased 40 acres on Romeo Plank Road just north of 21 Mile Road in Macomb Township in 1960. By 1972, Ray Sr. turned over the day-to-day operations to his sons Marvin, Philip, and Raymond. With Macomb Township's rapid growth in the early years, the business prospered. The nursery was expanded steadily and was eventually composed of eight divisions, with over 150 full-time employees on 800 acres in two locations for all the nursery stock. The wholesale yard, retail sales yard, and main offices are located here today. Ray Wiegand's Nursery celebrates its 77th anniversary in 2020. (Both, courtesy of the Ray Wiegand's Nursery collection.)

From approximately 1958 to 1989, Henry (also known as "Hank") and Janet Delmotte owned the Delmotte farm on Romeo Plank Road halfway between 21 Mile and 22 Mile Roads. Their home was located right across the road from the barbershop. This image is dated June 15, 1982. (Courtesy of the Larry and Christine Pretzer collection.)

Elizabeth Shotnik moved from Centerline, Michigan, after the death of her husband, Alosis, to Macomb Township, where she bought a farm on 22 Mile Road just east of Romeo Plank Road in 1969. Elizabeth had the help of her seven children on this farm. By 1975, the farm was sold for the development of a subdivision. (Courtesy of the Larry and Christine Pretzer collection.)

In 1948, Albert and Marie Malburg purchased their farm on 21 Mile Road between Card Road and North Avenue. The farm started out growing potatoes but eventually switched to mustard, turnip, and collard greens, cabbage, and head lettuce as its main crops. There were three rhubarb hothouses, and the produce was sold to the Eastern Market. Albert and Marie raised 12 children in this home—7 girls and 5 boys. It is now the site of the Woodberry subdivision. (Courtesy of the Karen Malburg Goodhue collection.)

This is a view of the dairy operations on the George and Clara Schroeder farm at 48000 Heydenreich Road. Shown at right is Gary Schroeder, age 13, feeding the cows, while his father Howard Schroeder (left), the farm's manager, examines herd records with county dairy agent John M. Burdick (center). This image was published with the article "Portrait of a Successful Dairy Farmer," by Edgar D. Racine, in the *Daily Monitor-Leader* on March 13, 1961. (Courtesy of the Mount Clemens Public Library collection.)

Seen here is an outside view of the Elmer and Ervin Glefke farm on Card Road near 22 Mile Road in Macomb Township. The brothers farmed an 80-acre homestead established by their great-grandparents Carl and Maria Glefke. This photograph was published with the news feature "Lack of Mechanization Fails to Hold Back Glefke Farmers" in the *Daily Monitor-Leader* on April 28, 1950. (Courtesy of the Mount Clemens Public Library collection.)

Pictured is the William Havel farm on Card Road in Macomb Township. Shown receiving a Centennial Farm plaque from Detroit Edison representative Dick Evans (right) are Marie Havel Ehrke (left) and Mrs. William Havel (center). The farm had been in the Havel family since 1852, and the house shown in this view was built in 1920. This image was published with the news feature "Two Farms Ready for Another Century," by G. Stuart DeMott, in the *Macomb Daily* on December 7, 1964. (Courtesy of the Mount Clemens Public Library collection.)

The Chippewa Valley School District was the recipient of the 44-acre farm that belonged to the late William and Dorothy Manthey on the southwest corner of 22 Mile Road and Garfield Road. In 1952, after William returned from serving in World War II, the couple purchased the property. William's job was teaching school in Detroit, and education was of the utmost importance to the couple. William was always firm about not selling to developers, so the gift they made to the school district was one way to continue his love of teaching. (Courtesy of the Andrew Andy Johnson collection.)

Milton Berz Jr., along with a few investors, built the Berz Macomb Airport in the late 1960s, and it opened for business in early 1970. Although an effort was made to put the airport into public ownership, the interest was not there. In 2002, an offer was made on the property by developers, and the decision was made to sell. The Berz family found their final day of operation on August 30, 2003—it was a tough one to get through. (Courtesy of the Jeff Berz collection.)

Ken Deneweth and Carolyn Kunkel married in 1962. They rented a small home from Ken's parents, Frank and Frances Deneweth, who truck gardened a 30-acre farm on 21 Mile Road in Utica, Michigan. Ken worked for his father on his farm, but his dream was for a farm of their own. In 1964, a 40-acre farm with no buildings was found, so a house was needed. With the bypass going through Utica, the couple placed a bid on a 1,100-square-foot white aluminum house with attached breezeway and garage. With the bid chosen, the house was moved from 23 Mile Road to its new location on the 40-acre farm on 22 Mile Road east of Hayes Road. Below is the "Deneweth's Pick Your Own" sign around 1975. (Both, courtesy of the Ken and Carolyn Deneweth collection.)

During those first years, supplemental jobs were needed to build the farm properly. Soon, there were wood-frame greenhouses behind the house to raise vegetable plants to grow in the fields. Cabbages, peppers, potatoes, and hot-house rhubarb were grown in the winter. Eventually, Ken was working the farm full-time. Over time, more greenhouses were added to grow the flowers that Carolyn loved so much. By 1978, their family was complete with five children, and soon, all the children learned the farming business. By 1995, Ken and Carolyn were ready to leave the business to sons Ken Jr. and Tom. Deneweth's continued to flourish. By 2007, the name was changed, and Deneweth's Garden Center was born. Pictured below around 1984 is Deneweth Farm with the Berz Macomb Airport in the distance. (Both, courtesy of the Ken and Carolyn Deneweth collection.)

By 1895, John Falkenhagen owned 80 acres of property on 22 Mile Road between Heydenreich and Card Roads. Forty acres were on the south side, and 40 acres were across the street on the north side of 22 Mile Road. John continued to work on this farm until sometime after 1925. John's daughter Carolyn Johanna Falkenhagen married Conrad Flory, and they started farming the 80-acre Flory property on Hall Road. (Courtesy of the John Eschenburg collection.)

Pictured is a gathering from 1925 of the Card family members on the William Card farm on 23 Mile Road and Card Road. From left to right are (first row) Jay, Earl Steinbrink, and Milton; (second row) Winefred, Elsa (holding Kenneth), Melvin (standing in the car), Eleanor, William, and Grace. (Courtesy of the Cynthia Donahue collection.)

This view shows the Eckert homestead on Romeo Plank Road and 23 Mile Road. Fred Eckert is pictured with his horse and buggy; perhaps he is waiting on his wife for a shopping trip in town. (Courtesy of the Macomb Township Historical Commission.)

John Miller and his wife, Emma Alwardt Miller, purchased a 95-acre farm on the southwest corner of 23 Mile Road and Card Road. In 1928, the Detroit Electric Company chose his farm to demonstrate the use of electric power on a farm, and his became the first all-electric farm in Macomb County. (Courtesy of the *Macomb Daily* and the Joy Raska Jennette collection.)

John and Emma Miller raised sons Harold and Norman and daughter Betty on this dairy farm. Below, Emma uses her new electric appliances, as everything at the farm was now powered by electricity: lights, milking machines, pumps, refrigerator, sweeper, fan, radio, water heater, poultry house, a water pump at the milk house for cooling the milk, and electric heat in the farmhouse. John went back to heating by either firewood or coal because the electric heat cost too much. (Both, courtesy of the *Macomb Daily* and the Joy Raska Jennette collection.)

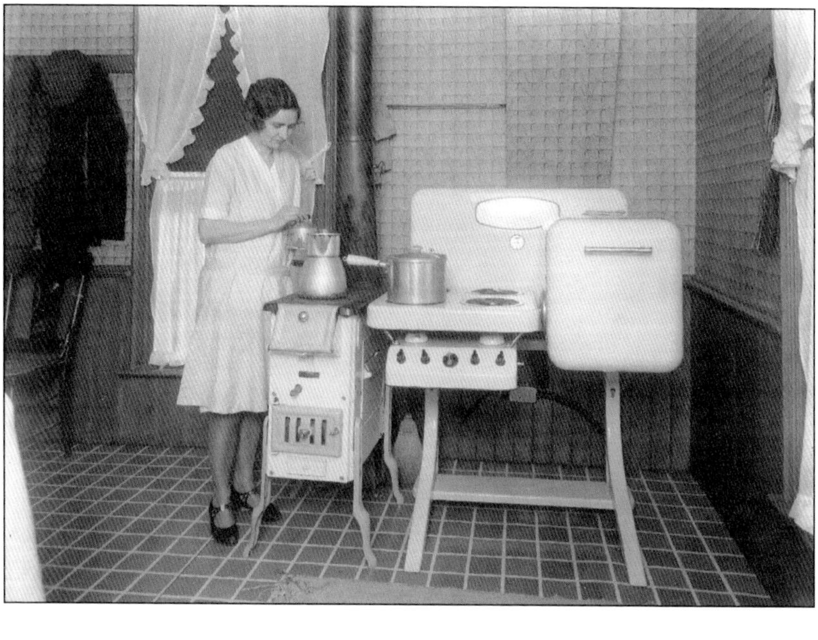

John Miller hoses down his silo. As seen below, the farm became the place for a huge annual picnic for farmers and their families to see the wonder of this modern development. His church, Immanuel Lutheran, sponsored a picnic lunch for the many people who attended. Card and 23 Mile Roads were dirt in those days, and 23 Mile Road had a different name. Miller said in an article from the *Macomb Daily* in 1988, "Our [east] side of Romeo Plank they called it Whiskey Road and on the other [west] side [of Romeo Plank Road], Cold Water Road. . . . On this side they drank whiskey, and on the other side they didn't." Miller was 99 years old when this article was written, and he said, "If you put that in the paper, they will all be moving to this side." (Both, courtesy of the *Macomb Daily* and the Joy Raska Jennett collection.)

Emil (1897–1991) and Antoinette (1901–1957) Meerschaert purchased a 64-acre property at 15291 23 Mile Road, on the northeast corner of 23 Mile and Hayes Roads, in 1945. They raised 11 children on the farm. Vegetables were the main produce, and the couple made trips down to the Eastern Market in Detroit to sell their crops. By the late 1980s, Emil sold the farm, and for a while, Kroger had a home on the property until the Emagine theater took over the space. (Both, courtesy of the Margaret Hessell collection.)

In 1957, Bob (1928–1985) and Mary Raska (1933–2001) purchased 15 acres on the northeast corner of 23 Mile and Romeo Plank Roads in Macomb. Here, they ran the business they started in 1954, Raska Trucking and Disposal. The property was sold in 1995. (Courtesy of the Joy Raska Jennett collection.)

Pictured is the farm of William and Clara Sans on 23 Mile Road east of Romeo Plank Road, by the middle branch of the Clinton River—what the locals called "the Crick"—just before the fire station on 23 Mile Road. (Courtesy of the Macomb Township Historical Commission.)

In 1911, Adam (1886–1974) and Victoria (1889–1966) Olejnik married, and they went on to have three children. In 1926, they purchased 40 acres on the north side of 23 Mile Road east of Card Road. They were considered truck farmers, as Adam and Victoria went to the various farm markets in the area, like Eastern Market, to sell their produce of corn, beans, watermelons, and cucumbers. (Both, courtesy of the Olejnik Farm collection.)

Adam and Victoria's son Chester (1921–2004), his wife, Lottie (1926–2014), and their seven children expanded the farm from 40 to 60 acres and soon had 23 greenhouses, where flowers were added to the many different types of produce they continued to sell. In 2020, the family saw the Olejnik Farm celebrate 94 years of serving their community. (Both, courtesy of the Olejnik Farm collection.)

Pictured is the Penzien farm property, located on the south side of 23 Mile Road east of Romeo Plank Road and the Crick. Joa Penzien and his workers take time off to pose for the photographer. (Courtesy of the Shelley Stier Henshaw collection.)

Leo's Tavern and Emporium was on North Avenue and 23 Mile Road in Macomb Township. A barbershop was located next to the restaurant/bar and gas station. A buzzer was hooked up in the bar area to make customers aware when one of the barbershop's six seats was ready for the next customer. Leo Mianeki tended the bar, and Pete Mianeki ran the gas station, making this a favorite meeting place for the locals. (Courtesy of the Cynthia Donahue collection.)

From left to right, Walt Klumfoot, Ed Schnieder, Roy Gerbel, and Harold Miller work on the Miller farm around 1941. To the right, Milt Miller relaxes with his dog on the Miller farm, located on 23 Mile Road east of North Avenue, around 1943. (Both, courtesy of the Milton Miller collection.)

The Harold Miller farm was located on 23 Mile Road east of North Avenue. Harold purchased the farm in 1935 from Daniel Shattuck. Eventually, Harold's son Milt took over the running of the farm. Shown below is the Robert Klockow farm, on the northwest corner of 23 Mile Road and North Avenue, around 1945. (Both, courtesy of the Milton Miller collection.)

Pictured are farming friends on a break around 1955. From left to right are (first row) Kenneth Roland; (second row) Bill Petzock, Walt Klumfoot, Milt Miller, Erv Schneider, Ed Schneider, Harold Miller, and Robert Klochow. (Courtesy of the Milton Miller collection.)

In the 1930s, Allen and Jessie Miller started a farm at 15771 24 Mile Road. This farm stretched to the northeast corner of 24 and Hayes Roads. As the years passed, the farm came into the care of their son George and daughter-in-law Donna Miller. The farm grew a number of different vegetables, especially asparagus. A switch was made to nursery stock for landscaping. During the 1930s and 1940s, there was a Massey Harris tractor dealership on the farm. Allen and Jessie's white farmhouse is still on 24 Mile Road, along with some of the barns. (Courtesy of the Dawn Miller collection.)

This photograph, taken on May 25, 1950, shows, from left to right, William Trapp, Mr. Dopp, William Stier, Mr. Scheibler, unidentified, Mr. Stade, Al Stark, and William Nahn taking a break while tilling the soil on the north side of 24 Mile Road west of Romeo Plank Road. (Courtesy of the Shelley Stier Henshaw collection.)

Louis P. Schoenherr (1906–1987) and Cecilia Theut Schoenherr (1908–1981) purchased a farm in 1940 at 19899 24 Mile Road between Romeo Plank and Foss Roads. They worked it as a dairy farm until 1962 and then changed over to vegetables and hot-house rhubarb, which was sold at the Eastern Market in Detroit until 1971. (Courtesy of the Pete Schoenherr collection.)

Louis and Cecilia's children—daughter Lois and sons Cecil, Clare, and Peter—helped out on the farm and continued to run it for a time after the death of their father. Above, Louis sits on his new 1953 Ford tractor, with son Peter directing him which way to go on his own tractor. In the image below, it appears Peter decided he might make more headway taking the lead on his own. (Both, courtesy of the Pete Schoenherr collection.)

Fred A. Eschenburg first appeared in the 1895 Macomb Township survey map, owning 80 areas of land in section 15 on Foss Road between 23 Mile and 24 Mile Roads. By 1916, that same land belonged to Paul Eschenburg. Fred A. Eschenburg had purchased C.W. Whitney's 119-acre property on 24 Mile Road and was attached to the Foss Road property. The Whitney Cemetery was in the northeast corner of his 24 Mile Road property. By 1925, these two parcels of land had been sold, and Fred had an 80-acre parcel on the north side of 24 Mile Road. These two mid-1890s photographs are of the Eschenburg barn raising. (Both, courtesy of the Macomb Township Historical Commission.)

Friedrich Johann Theodor Eschenburg (1856–1925) and Maria Carolyn Henrika Dohramm Eschenburg (1861–1941) gather their family around them around 1906. From left to right are (first row) Clara, Harry, Hilda, and Alma; (second row) Lily, Henry "Hank," Friedrich (holding Metha), Marie, Frederick "Fred" A., and Marie; (third row) Carl, Wilhelm "Bill," Minnie, Paul, and John. Friedrich Eschenburg purchased the property on 24 Mile Road in 1891. Below, Friedrich (left) and his brother Carl, along with their wives, are seen in this c. 1920 photograph. (Both, courtesy of the John Eschenburg collection.)

Charles Schramm was born in Waldeck, Germany, in 1849. His family came to America in 1854 and settled on a farm in the 22 Mile and Heindrick Roads area of Macomb Township. In 1873, he married Fredericka Kath and bought a farm next to his parents' home. By the mid-1880s, Charles moved his family of 11 children to a farm next door to his son Robert at 21811 24 Mile Road. This farm stayed in the same family and became a Centennial Farm in 2011. (Courtesy of the Schramm family collection.)

Robert Schramm purchased 30 acres from Charles and Frank Stroup on March 14, 1908. Robert married Ida Marie Siewert on February 23, 1909, and they and their eight children made their home at 21701 24 Mile Road. (Courtesy of the Schramm family collection.)

The house had windows with several panes and a small porch in the center front. Two black walnut trees grew along the unpaved 24 Mile Road and still grace the road at the present time. (Courtesy of the Schramm family collection.)

Pictured is the Robert and Ida Schramm family. From left to right are (first row) Irene, Ervin, Beatrice, and Evelyn; (second row) Martin, Robert, Ida, Martha, and Gertrude. (Courtesy of the Schramm family collection.)

For many years, Robert was a charter member of the United Dairy Farmers, and he never missed a meeting. A news article printed in the *United Dairy Farmer* on June 15, 1942, featured a story about Robert and Ida Schramm, who won the old-time waltzing contest at the Dairy Farmers' party, held in Waldenburg, Michigan. (Courtesy of the Schramm family collection.)

Martin and Esther Schramm purchased the farm from the family estate on March 4, 1963. They continued to live at the 21811 24 Mile Road farm. The family raised milk cows and grew grains and corn. Their son Kenneth stayed on the farm and helped his parents look after the 180 acres. In 1970, the house took on a new look, with new windows and siding. (Courtesy of the Schramm family collection.)

Kenneth and May Schramm purchased the farm from Martin and Ester on September 24, 1990. They were married on July 2, 1966, lived in the family home, and raised five children. As the family continued to farm, their son Thomas joined in as a third-generation farmer of this family land. They milked cows and grew grains, straw, and hay. Eggs, fruit, and vegetables were still sold at the market, with the dairy cows being sold in 2002. Pictured below is a gathering of the Kenneth and May Schramm family to celebrate the 2012 centennial celebration of the farm. (Both, courtesy of the Schramm family collection.)

Whitney Cemetery, also called Macomb Center Cemetery, is located on 24 Mile Road between Foss and Card Roads. The land originally belonged to John Whitney. Many early residents of this area found their resting place in the Whitney Cemetery, including the Cards, Eschenburgs, Fosses, Schramms, Stroups, and Whitneys. (Both, author's collection.)

Two

WALDENBURG, MACOMB CORNERS, AND MEADE

In the early 1800s, there were three Waldenburgs along Romeo Plank Road. South Waldenburg was at Hall Road (Michigan Highway 59 today). It had the former Trinity Lutheran Church and cemetery. Later on, the corner was Bobceans grocery and gas station, a bar, and a dance hall. One mile north was the original Waldenburg, where Immanuel Lutheran Church is located. North Waldenburg was one more mile farther, at 22 Mile Road. This aerial image shows 22 Mile Road (Waldenburg Road) and Romeo Plank Road. (Courtesy of the Shelley Stier Henshaw collection.)

Waldenburg, a small, unincorporated town in Macomb Township, was first settled in 1831. It was a German settlement of immigrants mainly from Prussia. The settlers liked the idea of settling where there was water available in the middle branch of the Clinton River, which was always called the Crick (Creek) by its inhabitants. Below, a 1900 postal code is seen on this postcard, when Waldenburg had a postal station of its own. That ended shortly after the first part of the 1900s. (Both, courtesy of the Shelley Stier Henshaw collection.)

In this image is the Ambrose and Augusta Leyer residence, located at 49185 Romeo Plank Road. From left to right are unidentified, Theodore Leyer, Augusta Leyer, two unidentified, and Ambrose Leyer. (Courtesy of the Shelley Stier Henshaw collection.)

Pictured here is a family reunion. From left to right are (first row) Albert Kruth, Willie Kruth, Prince, Walter Stier and Arnold Kruth; (second row) Aurelia Kramer, Elsie Kramer, Myrtle Stier, Elise Stier (with Ruth on her lap), Grandfather Dopp (with Wilbur on his lap), Howard, Grandmother Dopp, and Fred; (third row) Emma Kramer, Charlie Kramer, Lena Bellman, Charlie Bellman, Sophia and ? Kruth, Bill Stier, Bertha, and Rob Dopp. (Courtesy of the Shelley Stier Henshaw collection.)

The Peters and Kruth General Store sat on the northwest corner of 22 Mile Road facing Romeo Plank Road. The store burned down about 1906–1908, caused by overheated gas lights in the kitchen, located in the back of the stairs. The owner at the time of this photograph was August Peters. From left to right are John Peters and his adopted daughter Augusta Leyer (who worked in the store), Mrs. Peters (seated), and Mr. Peters. Later owners were the Trapp and Kruth families. (Courtesy of the Shelley Stier Henshaw collection.)

Pictured is the William Liebig/Johann Christian Rewoldt farm, located on the west side of Romeo Plank Road north of 22 Mile Road, on the edge of the village of Waldenburg. The home was originally built by Wilhelm Liebig and his wife, Rosanna Tietze Liebig, who passed on ownership to William Sperlich and Marie Liebig. When William Sperlich was killed in a train accident, his widow, Marie, married fellow widower Johann Rewoldt. The farm property was leased to the Detroit Creamery Company to raise milk cows. The house still stands today. (Courtesy of the Mount Clemens Public Library collection.)

Ambrose Leyer was born on March 30, 1840, in Austrian Silesia. He was apprenticed to a trade, and he selected the art of cobbling. Ambrose's uncle August Posner came to Waldenburg and established a brickyard and potash factory. Grieved that his Lutheran church did not have a musical instrument to enliven the service, he found that his old church in Silesia had discarded its old trombone. A $35 charge was made, and Leyer brought the musical instrument to Waldenburg. (Courtesy of the Shelley Stier Henshaw collection.)

Upon his arrival, Ambrose "took up" 10 acres near the north end of Waldenburg. His home and cobbler shop were located in an abandoned toll gate of the Romeo Plank Road Company. He also farmed his land. The cobbler of Waldenburg married and reared nine children. He lived until his 93rd year, declaring that whiskey was medicine if used properly. He died on March 30, 1933. His daughter Fredericka, after becoming a widow, married William Stier, also a widower, in 1945 or 1946. They made their home in the Leyer house. (Courtesy of the Shelley Stier Henshaw collection.)

George Stier (1823–1918) moved his family to Macomb Township in 1857. The house at 49185 Romeo Plank Road was on the west side of the road, and the 40 acres of farmland was on the east side. It was an even half-mile between Waldenburg Road (22 Mile Road) and Whiskey Road (23 Mile Road). George passed away in Waldenburg in 1918 at the young age of 94 years. This photograph of George and Bertha Stier was taken in Waldenburg, Germany, prior to immigrating. (Courtesy of the Shelley Stier Henshaw collection.)

George Wilhelm Ludwig "Louis" Stier married Bertha Eiheim at Immanuel Lutheran in 1878. They raised seven children and took over the 40-acre farm belonging to Bertha's parents on the southeast corner of 22 Mile and Romeo Plank Roads. The house and barn stood until 2004, when they were torn down to build the Waldenburg Plaza. From left to right are (first row) Albert Stier, Louis Stier, Clarence Stier, Bertha Stier, and William Stier; (second row) Emma Stier, Elizabeth Stier, Martha Stier, and Helen Stier. (Courtesy of the Shelley Stier Henshaw collection.)

As well as farming, Louis Stier established Stier Hardware in 1903 in a former post office building. The Steyers added small buildings over time and put them all together to create the one large building that stood on the corner of 22 Mile and Romeo Plank Roads. Stier Hardware, in its heyday, carried everything its customers could think of needing. Louis's great-granddaughter Shelley Stier Henshaw remembered living in an 800-square-foot apartment at one end of the store with her family. By the time Shelley was 11 or 12, she could put her hand into the nail bucket and come up with exactly a pound of nails. (Both, courtesy of the Shelley Stier Henshaw collection.)

Seen at L. Stier and Sons around 1916 are, from left to right, unidentified, Albert Stier, Holdreich Grosser, Magdalena Stier, Gertrude Stier, Edward Stier, "Pa" William Stier, Bertha Dopp, Robb Dopp, unidentified (listed on the photograph as "his grandfather"), and Bill Stier (with the Model T). Seen below, William Stier, Louis's son, took over the business and then handed it down to Shelley's father, Carl Stier, in 1950. The hardware eventually expanded to carry gifts and toys and offered a layaway plan. (Both, courtesy of the Shelley Stier Henshaw collection.)

By 2013, the Stier Hardware at 48980 Romeo Plank Road had to be torn down. The store had been closed for a number of years and was deemed unsafe by township officials. The township needed the site for a widening of Romeo Plank Road, and the building that much of the community had used or seen over the years needed to be torn down to make way for that progress. (Courtesy of the Shelley Stier Henshaw collection.)

Waldenburg Feed and Gas Station was run by Ralph Stade. There he stored a large volume of cattle feed and fertilizers and carried tires and other items of use to the local farmers; it eventually became a service station. (Courtesy of the Shelley Stier Henshaw collection.)

After the Peters and Kruth General Store burned down, Robert Dopp bought the land and, in 1908, began construction on a new store. By 1909, the store was taking shape. The capstone today still reads "1909." (Courtesy of the Shelley Stier Henshaw collection.)

When completed, the Dopp store included groceries and clothing on the main floor as well as an area for furniture sales. Ford automobile sales took up the second floor. Later, the furniture store was out and a dance floor came in. The Heidelberg Eight band came from Germany and played "good" German dance music, much to the satisfaction of all who attended. (Courtesy of the Shelley Stier Henshaw collection.)

Robert Dopp sold his interest in the property and moved to Canada. Charles Stade bought out his interest, and soon, the time came for the dance hall to depart, as it became more lucrative for Stade to remodel the second floor into apartments. He found plenty of tenants from Selfridge Air Base needing places to live. (Courtesy of the Shelley Stier Henshaw collection.)

Charles Stade's son Leon bought the grocery store business, which included a soda fountain, from Charles Colparet. The clothing department and tavern had now vacated the building, so another remodeling began to add apartments where the Stade sons lived for a time. In later times, the basement was partly remodeled into a meeting place, and as years moved on, several businesses operated from this building. This view is from around the 1980s. (Courtesy of the Shelley Stier Henshaw collection.)

Pictured is the Waldenburg baseball team; from left to right are (first row) Hugo Leitz, August Luchtman, Art Luchtman, and Ed McDonald; (second row) Walter Behm, Robert Posner, Ernest Eschenburg, Walter Jasmund, Hulde Grosser, Art Leitz, Hugo Grosser, and Gust Blohm. It was known that the pitcher, Art Luchtman, had the use of only one arm. (Courtesy of the Shelley Stier Henshaw collection.)

A group of workers takes a break from the construction of the Dopp Building in 1908 or 1909; included within this group are Louis Stier, William Stier, Clarence Stier, and William Trapp. Their sign reads "Local Option Enforced." A local option allowed the inhabitants of a community to restrict or outlaw the sale of alcohol. Did they become a dry community, or was it just tongue-in-cheek posturing for the photographer? (Courtesy of the Shelley Stier Henshaw collection.)

Here are two examples of Waldenburg postcards (also known as *Postkartes* or *cartes postales*), with the one below sent from Waldenburg to Mount Clemens on August 4, 1912, using a 1¢ postage stamp. Soon after, there was no longer a Waldenburg postal code to be used. (Both, courtesy of the Larry and Christine Pretzer collection.)

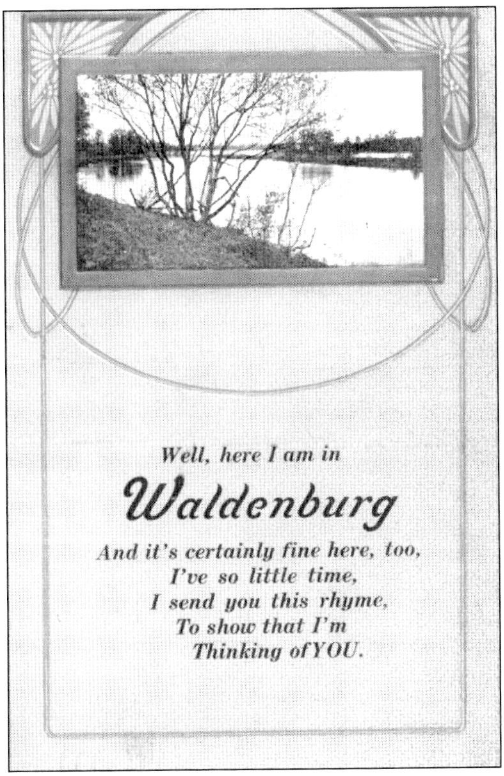

Robert Dopp's son Wilbur decided to start the Waldenburg Tavern in the Dopp Building. When Wilbur Dopp started a beer distributorship, he sold his interest to John Wittrig. Wittrig soon sold to Roy Dietrich. Dietrich moved across the street and bought land from the Stiers to erect his own larger building and, in 1948, moved the tavern there. Alvin Stark purchased the Waldenburg Tavern/Bar in 1971, and since then, three generations of Starks have owned and operated this long-established local for the farmers as well as the young suburbanites that rely on it now. (Courtesy of the Shelley Stier Henshaw collection.)

This early 1960s view of Romeo Plank Road looks south toward 22 Mile Road in the village of Waldenburg. Starting at the bottom right corner on the right side of the street are the Dopp family home, Ralph and Geraldine Stade's feed store, and the Dopp Bros. store. Across 22 Mile Road is Rohrbeck's Market. On the left side of the street are Wilburt and Ethel Harder's home, Byron and Amanda Weisskirch's home, and Wilbur and Pearl Dopp's home. (Courtesy of the Mount Clemens Public Library collection.)

Daniel Miller was born on February 18, 1798, in Madison County, New York. In 1818, he married Lucinda Hurlburt and relocated to Washington Township, where he spent 10 years working on a farm. He received land grants from his service in the War of 1812. He then bought nearly 200 acres in Macomb Township, where he resided for the next 30 years. His wife passed away in 1842, leaving behind four children. Daniel's son Nelson Hurlburt Miller (1832–1916) took over the farm when Daniel moved to Romeo and bought a home on Benjamin Street in 1869. Daniel married two additional times before his death on September 16, 1889, in Macomb Township, Michigan. (Courtesy of the Mike Ellis family collection.)

There was a sawmill operation on the Daniel H. Miller farm, located on 25 Mile Road east of Romeo Plank Road. Daniel H. Miller was born on December 24, 1873, to Nelson and Caroline Dixon Miller, early pioneers of the county. He operated the sawmill for over 60 years until his death on January 3, 1956. During its peak years of operation, the Miller sawmill provided sawn lumber to the Donaldson Brothers firm in Mount Clemens for the production of sleighs, carriages, and wagons. On December 17, 1948, the *Daily Monitor-Leader* ran a feature story by Harold C. Engelman on the farm titled "75-Year-Old Farmer Still Active in Sawmill Operation." (Courtesy of the Mount Clemens Public Library collection.)

Noble Robert Sutton was born on February 18, 1821, in Monroe County, New York. After his father's early death, he came to Macomb Township with his mother and elder brother, and he bought 60 acres of land on section 8, on the south side of Romeo Plank Road in the area of Macomb Corners. In October 1844, he married Marion Maria Miller, a daughter of Daniel Miller, his neighbor. (Courtesy of the Mike Ellis family collection.)

Pictured is the Noble Sutton home. Starting in 1853, Noble kept a tollgate in Mount Clemens at Romeo Plank Road for two years, and he returned to the farm in 1856. The original Sutton home was located about a mile west of Macomb Corners. Noble Sutton passed away in Coldwater, Branch County, Michigan, on January 18, 1892. (Courtesy of the Mike Ellis family collection.)

Marion Maria Miller, daughter of Daniel Miller and Lucinda Hurlburt, was born on August 16, 1828, in Washington, Michigan. She married Noble Robert Sutton on October 3, 1844. Here, Marion holds daughter Mary Arabelle Sutton (born January 29, 1850), who grew up to marry Theodore Marshall Giddings. Below is a view of the Sutton homestead on Runyon Road, known now as 25 Mile Road. (Both, courtesy of the Mike Ellis family collection.)

William and Emma Penzien, parents of Joachim "Joa" Penzien (1914–2011), purchased the farm at 25 Mile Road and Romeo Plank Road in 1911 from the Miller family, who had been the original owners of the property since 1831. In the 1930s, William's sons, William, Joa, and Arthur, with hard work and improvement, transitioned from dairy farming and grain crops to growing vegetables that they, like many of their neighbors, took to the Eastern Market in Detroit. (Above, courtesy of the Diane Penzien collection; below, courtesy of the James Arthur Penzien collection.)

In 1942, William Jr. and Arthur left the farm to Joa. The same year, Joa married Beatrice Bock (1922–2012), and they continued with the expansion of the farm. Joa and his sons, Jim and Richard, started to grow potatoes in the sandy loam on the farm. Soon, Joa earned the nickname "Mr. Potato" due to his innovations in the farming business. With better and more efficient equipment and the introduction of herbicides, his produce really increased. (Both, courtesy of the James Arthur Penzien collection.)

At one point in time, Penzien Farms covered some 315 acres in Macomb Township. Outside of farming, Penzien was deeply involved in his community. He maintained an active role in the township government by serving as a member of the township's planning commission for some 20 years. (Courtesy of the Andrew Andy Johnson collection.)

Joa was one of the original developers of the Wolverine Golf Course, known as the first golf course in Macomb Township, on 25 Mile and Romeo Plank Roads. Later on, Joa developed the Cracklewood Golf Course on 24 Mile Road east of Romeo Plank Road. He passed away at the age of 99 in 2011, leaving behind a legacy his family could be proud of. (Courtesy of the Andrew Andy Johnson collection.)

One afternoon in August 1961, the barn on Doris Goodhue, of 18721 25 Mile Road in Macomb Township, burned to the ground. The family lost a cow and a small puppy; their tractor and 600 bales of hay were also destroyed. With the death by heart attack of her husband Harley two months previously, Doris had been getting help from family members and her eight children. Her thoughts turned to a firefighter who would recover but was still gravely hurt. From left to right are (first row) Susan, Marlene, Diane (holding Randy), and Rickie; (second row) Mickey (holding the puppy) and Dale. Gerald, the 14-year-old son, modestly refused to appear in this image, published in the *Daily Monitor-Leader* on Friday, August 11, 1961. (Courtesy of the Diane Penzien collection.)

Art Penzien and his wife, Irma Ries Penzien, had the only "non-farm house" in the area, although the property was surrounded by his brother Joa's potato crops. He worked outside the farming industry for most of his adult life. Their home on Romeo Plank Road was between 25 Mile and 24 Mile Roads. (Courtesy of the Diane Penzien collection.)

Leo (1923–2000) Hellebuyck and his wife, Marcella (1925–2019), purchased a farm at 18850 25 Mile Road in the area of Macomb Corners and raised their five children there. They were truck farmers who sold their produce of strawberries, raspberries, and assorted types of melons at the Eastern Market while maintaining a "Pick Your Own" program on the farm itself. In the winter, they grew hot-house rhubarb in the greenhouse to sell at the market. (Courtesy of the Carol Roose family collection.)

Edward Kreger owned a 130-acre-diary farm on the north side of 25 Mile Road where Romeo Plank Road made it necessary to make either a right or a left turn. He was approached in the mid-1960s to sell his land to create the first golf course in Macomb Township, and with help from his friend Joa Penzien, the Wolverine Golf Course came into being. (Courtesy of the Macomb Township Historical Commission.)

William C. Schoof (1889–1959) and Ella Kuechenmeister (1889–1957) married in 1912. They worked their farm at 25 Mile and Romeo Plank Roads. William was known as one of only three master farmers in Macomb County, where his Holstein cows were the pride of his dairy farm. Below, this image of Ella's parlor shows the new electric lighting that Detroit Edison had put into the house. (Both, courtesy of the Jeff Altermatt collection.)

With William Schoof's farm being one of a few newly electric farms in the area, Detroit Edison came out periodically and took pictures to show the convenience of the electricity. Schoof is pictured adding water to his new Easaway seven-gallon-capacity gravity-type water heater around 1940. Below, he fills the silo with his corn produce around 1931. (Both, courtesy of the Jeff Altermatt collection.)

March, 1950 HOLSTEIN MICHIGANDER Page 11

A DIFFICULT DECISION - BUT IT ALL GOES

On Saturday, April 1, 1950, at 12:00 noon, on the Wm. C. Schoof Farm located in Macomb County, Mich. (25 Mile Road at the Romeo Road)

As I have quit farming and am moving to Mt. Clemens, I will offer at Public Auction my herd of Holsteins and everything for the Dairy Farmer. Included in this lot are 2 yearling bulls. Robdale Illehee Sovereign—his dam has 683 Fat. A beautiful grandson of Sovereign. Robdale Sylv-O-Fayne, grandson of Monogram—his 3 nearest dams average 782 Fat.

All the farm machinery, equipment, and Homestead, including several beautiful well kept buildings. 120 acres of land with 26 acres in wheat. The rest all plowed for spring planting.

Only Three Master Farmers in Macomb County
. . . and William C. Schoof is one of these.

The Old Homestead (above) has a 7 room house, bath, utility room, and excellent well water.

W. C. SCHOOF

Washington, Michigan - Phone 3966

C. B. SMITH, Auctioneer **MORRIS C. PLACE, Clerk**

It was a difficult decision for William Schoof, but on April 1, 1950, at 12:00 p.m., he put his farm at 25 Mile and Romeo Plank Roads up for auction. He planned to sell his herd of Holsteins and everything that the future dairy farmer would need, including his 120 acres of land with 26 acres in wheat and all fields plowed and ready for the spring planting. Included in the auction was his homestead, located at 4415 Runyon Road (25 Mile Road). (Courtesy of the Jeff Altermatt collection.)

Joseph Altermatt came to Macomb Township from a farm in Warren Township and purchased his new farm at 4415 Runyon Road and Romeo Plank Road in Macomb Corners. He was considered a truck farmer, as he and his family drove their produce down to the Eastern Market in Detroit to sell. In the winter, Joseph grew hot-house rhubarb and also took that to market. When Joseph retired, his son John and John's wife, Darlene, took over the running of the farm. By the late 1990s, John's son Jeff and Jeff's sisters Lynne, Renee, and Jennifer became the managing owners of the farm, with John continuing to supervise the operation. Below, Joseph and his daughter Margaret hold a box of their hot-house rhubarb. (Both, courtesy of the Jeff Altermatt collection.)

John Altermatt holds a farm sign showing that strawberries were for sale at the farm market. The Detroit Eastern Market was an important part of the history for those farmers that depended on income from specialty crops such as fruits and vegetables, commonly known as "truck gardeners." Below is the produce sign for the Altermatt & Sons farm. The farm's address started in Washington and moved to Macomb when the postal system changed. At one point in time, it was mandatory to display these signs when selling at the market. (Both, courtesy of the Jeff Altermatt collection.)

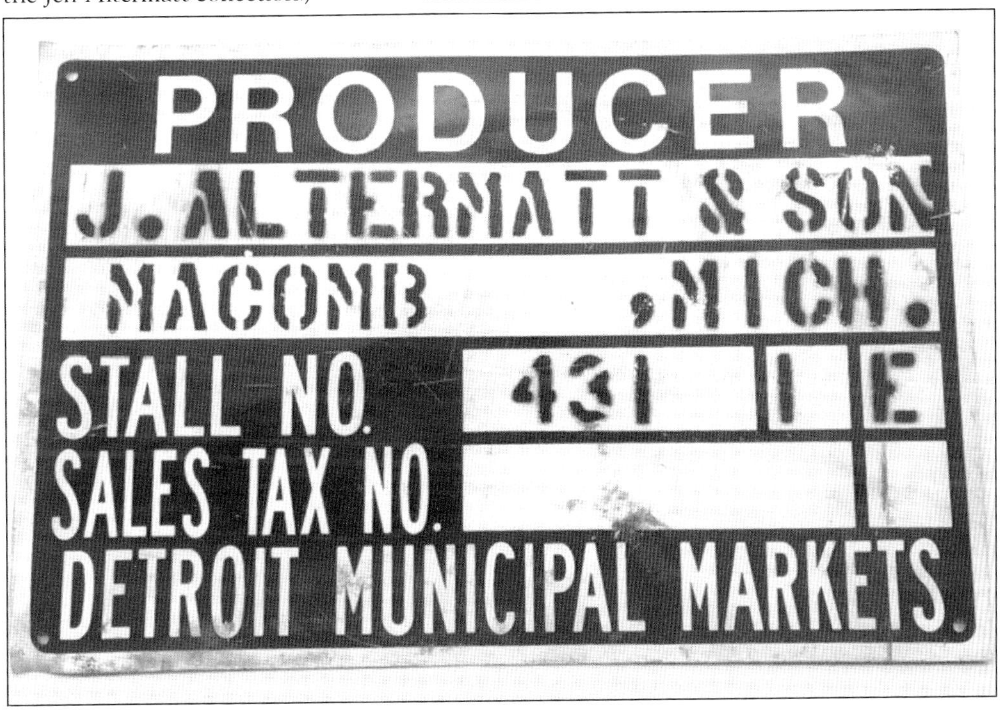

George Rang (1881–1977) married Elizabeth Schoof (1887–1980) from the neighboring farm on April 15, 1909, in Macomb Township, Michigan. By 1916, they owned a 72-acre dairy farm on the west side of Romeo Plank Road south of the bridge. (Courtesy of the Bill Rang collection.)

George took the milk in cans by horse and wagon to Detroit. He usually spent the night at Half Way, a lodging place that is now in Eastpoint, halfway between Detroit and Macomb Township. At that time, Romeo Plank Road was paved with planks, making for an easier ride. Seen here is Don Rang, George and Lizzie's son, with their horses King and Queen around the 1940s. (Courtesy of the Bill Rang collection.)

By the late 1940s, George had his two sons, Stewart and Donald, running the farming business but found that it was hard to support two families. Donald worked for Macomb County for the next 30 years, and Stewart stayed with the farm. Here, Bill, George's grandson, shows the photographer the muscles he gained from working the farm. (Courtesy of the Bill Rang collection.)

By the time George passed away in 1977, he and Lizzie had been married for 68 years; Lizzie passed in 1980. They were both buried in St. Peter Cemetery. Soon after, the property was divided up and sold to developers. (Courtesy of the Bill Rang collection.)

In 1905, the Christian Association chose the name St. John's German Evangelical Church for the church located on the northeast corner of Romeo Plank and 25 Mile Roads. A group of parishioners from St. Peter, a mile south of Macomb Corners, took the opportunity to start its own church, because the members wanted to join the old Gleaners Hall. In 1951, it was voted to dissolve the St. John's congregation, and the property was sold. A fund was established for the perpetual care of the St. John's Cemetery Association, located two miles west of Macomb Corners. The former church went on to be known as the Lutheran Fraternities of America (LFA) Hall, where gatherings and receptions made good use of the revered building. Below, the Silver House Market, known in the past by many names, such as Meyers Market, Clem's Market, and the D&M Market, is still standing and helping the community today. (Above, courtesy of the Shelley Stier Henshaw collection; below, courtesy of the author's collection.)

The community changed its name to Meade in 1863 after Gen. George Gordon Meade during the American Civil War but remained locally known as the Crawford Settlement. Meade encompassed two communities, one north of 26 Mile Road in Ray Township and one south of 26 Mile Road in Macomb Township. W.D. Begrow's was a grocery and dry goods shop on the southeast corner of 23 Mile Road and North Avenue. (Both, courtesy of the Friends of the Ray Township Library.)

The Lefurgey Service and Hardware Store was located at 56975 North Avenue, New Haven, on the southwest corner of 26 Mile Road and North Avenue. It was known to give "Quality service—in the family tradition" and for plumbing supplies, hardware, groceries, and Union 76 gas. (Courtesy of the Friends of the Ray Township Library.)

Seen here is Harry Lefurgey, of the village of Meade in Macomb Township, standing beside a Michigan Centennial Farm marker on his land. The farm, at 56881 North Avenue, is just south of 26 Mile Road and has been in the Lefurgey family since 1845. This image was published with the news feature "Meade Traces Its History to the Farmers," by Robert Selwa, in the *Macomb Daily* on November 12, 1985. (Courtesy of the Mount Clemens Public Library collection.)

Paul Blonde, born in 1889 in a farming village in France, came to the United States and settled in the village of Meade in the early part of the 20th century. He went to work at the Meade Creamery during the horse-and-buggy days of Macomb Township, starting in 1915. There were 25 to 30 farmers who brought their milk to the creamery, where they separated the cream and milk. Meade Creamery was a substation for the Chesterfield Creamery, and the cream was hauled over to Chesterfield. Below, freight is moved on the rough 26 Mile Road in Meade. (Above, courtesy of the Friends of the Ray Township Library; below, courtesy of the Cynthia Donahue collection.)

Meade Cemetery is located on 26 Mile Road west of Omo Road in Macomb Township. Revolutionary War veteran John Crawford and his wife, Ann, founded this cemetery in 1837. Veterans of every major war since the American Revolution are buried here. Many local residents found their resting places in this cemetery, including the Crawfords, Dursts, Fosses, Klusendorfs, and Schroeders, among others. (Both, author's collection.)

Three

Macomb Township Services

The original Macomb Township Hall, at 19925 23 Mile Road, was built in 1919 and served the township until a new hall was erected at the same location in 1974. The cost to build the original hall was $1,600. The old hall was sold to a private buyer and removed from the site. This photograph appeared in the *Daily Monitor-Leader* on August 16, 1963. (Courtesy of the Mount Clemens Public Library collection.)

This front view of the first township hall and the surrounding farmlands appeared in the *Daily Monitor-Leader* on August 16, 1963. Below, the *Macomb Daily* came out on February 8, 1974, to capture both of the township halls: the one no longer in use and the hall that came in at the cost of $70,000 and was now able to handle the growth that was coming to the fast-growing community of Macomb Township. (Both, courtesy of the Mount Clemens Public Library collection.)

Pictured at the dedication ceremony for the new Macomb Township Hall are, from left to right, Lion's Club representative Milton Miller, township treasurer Marvin Blank, supervisor Ronald DeBuck, circuit court judge George R. Deneweth, and Macomb County commissioner Walter Franchuk of District 3. This image was published with the news article "Officials Gather to Dedicate Hall" in the *Macomb Daily* on February 10, 1974. (Courtesy of the Mount Clemens Public Library collection.)

Pictured are two future treasurers of Macomb Township. Marie Malburg holds her daughter Karen in 1950. They had a farm at 21 Mile and Card Roads. Marie was the township treasurer from 1988 to 2009, and her daughter Karen Goodhue followed as treasurer from 2009 to today. (Courtesy of the Karen Goodhue collection.)

The Macomb Township Volunteer Fire Department is seen here around 1953, about the same time it officially came into existence. The farmers played a critical role just by being available at home and having a telephone. The department used people who were more or less available 24 hours a day. The first person who arrived at the fire hall sounded the siren to summon the volunteers throughout the township. Equipment purchases in the mid-1950s required firefighters to solicit money door to door to buy a pumper at the outrageous price of about $750. Below is a formal group photograph of the new department. In 2003, the department celebrated 50 years, still operating much like it did in 1953. (Both, courtesy of the Macomb Township Historical Commission.)

Seen here is the Macomb Township Fire Department. From left to right are Marvin Blank, Elmer Sudau, Martin Schramm, Russ Koss, and Joe Koss, the fire chief. Station 1 was decommissioned and demolished in 2020 after 68 years of service to the community. (Courtesy of the Macomb Township Historical Commission.)

Seen here is the exterior view of the Macomb Township Fire Hall at 23 Mile and Romeo Plank Roads. Charter members of the township's volunteer department pose with their new GMC Firemaster pumper truck. Shown fourth and fifth from the left in front of the truck are township attorney George R. Deneweth and supervisor Paul Bock. This image was published with the article "Township Gets First Fire Truck, Hall and Volunteers" in the *Daily Monitor-Leader* on March 31, 1953. (Courtesy of the Mount Clemens Public Library collection.)

Harold Rohrbeck (1917–1974) was one of the many township farmers who worked to get the Macomb Township Fire Department up and running in the early 1950s. While tending his farm, where he raised cows and chickens, he helped with his brother-in-law's gas station while juggling fireman duties. He eventually worked work for the Macomb County Road Commission until his passing. His son Karl, who followed his father and joined the fire department, passed away in 2019. Among the belongings left behind was Harold's precious badge, seen below. (Both, courtesy of the Diane Rohrbeck Frank collection.)

Four

Schools and Churches

The Meade School, built in 1837, was in the Vienna Settlement, as it was known then; the settlement was still part of both Chesterfield Township and Macomb Township during that time. There was not a separation of the two communities until 1842. Meade School was located on Fairchild Road south of 26 Mile Road and is now a private home. (Courtesy of the Friends of the Ray Township Library.)

The Atwood School, in Macomb Township Fractional District No. 1, was located at 45690 North Avenue. This photograph was published with "Mothers Club Supports School Programs," by Harold C. Engelman, in the *Daily Monitor-Leader* on April 22, 1949. (Courtesy of the Mount Clemens Public Library collection.)

The Berger School, in Macomb Township, was a one-room school that served School District No. 2 in Macomb and Shelby Townships. The building was located on the southwest corner of Romeo Plank and 23 Mile Roads. The first Berger School was built in 1870, burned to the ground in 1933, and then was rebuilt several more times, finally ending up as the structure shown here. This image accompanied "One Room School Doomed" in the *Daily Monitor-Leader* on October 26, 1955. (Courtesy of the Mount Clemens Public Library collection.)

In 1956, a room was added to the Berger School as a second classroom. Teacher Oila Belle Wilson is shown holding the door for the students. The bell tower on the school is now at Big Stone School in New Baltimore. This image appeared with the news item "One-Room School is Now Two" in the *Daily Monitor-Leader* on March 6, 1956. (Courtesy of the Mount Clemens Public Library collection.)

This interior view of the Berger School was also taken from the article "One-Room School Doomed." (Courtesy of the Mount Clemens Public Library collection.)

The image above shows the Brick School class of 1929, and below is the Brick School class of 1936. No list of student names is available. (Both, courtesy of the Macomb Township Historical Commission.)

The Brick School, located on North Avenue halfway between 23 and 24 Mile Roads, is seen here in 1936. Pictured are Ed Yaeck (left) and Don Yaeck. (Courtesy of the Macomb Township Historical Commission.)

This is a Brick School class photograph from 1939. No list of student names is available. (Courtesy of the Macomb Township Historical Commission.)

The Card School, established in 1870, is now a private home at 49470 Card Road, Macomb Township, between 22 Mile and 23 Mile Roads. (Courtesy of the Cynthia Donahue collection.)

The Hartway School was located on Fairchild Road between 22 and 23 Mile Roads. Shown here is a class photograph from 1936. No list of student names is available. (Courtesy of the Macomb Township Historical Commission.)

The Macomb Corners School is pictured in 1952. The teacher is Lylia Smith. The students include Joyce Eschenburg, Joyce Thurp, Nancy Schwark, Bill Wurt, Jerry Boling, Bob Hopp, Dave Swark, Leroy Hopp, Maurice Hellebuyck, Sally Eschenburg, Archie Dewitt, Roy Rang, Sharon Boling, Bonnie Schwark, Julia Hellebuyck, Jim ?, Bill Eschenburg, and Tom Hopp. (Courtesy of the Macomb Township Historical Commission.)

Seen here is an exterior view of the former Meade School building on Omo Road south of 26 Mile Road in Macomb Township after it had been converted to a private residence. The school was built about 1868 and was converted to private use in 1968. This image appeared with "Old Schoolhouse Becomes Family Dream Come True," by Rosemary Vocino, in the *Macomb Daily* on November 9, 1972. (Courtesy of the Mount Clemens Public Library collection.)

Pictured here is the Meade School, on Omo Road south of 26 Mile Road. This photograph accompanied the article "Back-to-School Trek begins for Thousands of Macomb Youngsters of All Ages" in the *Daily Monitor-Leader* on September 5, 1950. (Courtesy of the Mount Clemens Public Library collection.)

Members of the Meade Farmerettes are shown working on a clean-up project to prepare the schoolhouse for a new school year. From left to right are Hazel Dodds, Doris Honert, and Sally Furton. This image was published with "A Clean School to Finance Winter Plans," by Arnold Bransdorfer, in the *Daily Monitor-Leader* on September 1, 1950. (Courtesy of the Mount Clemens Public Library collection.)

On February 7, 1966, representatives from 38 congregations in Oakland and Macomb Counties met and formed membership, site, and finance committees. They also passed a resolution to form the Lutheran High School North Committee. In the school's first year, 77 students enrolled for its first academic year. It opened in September 1972 and operated for a short time in the former day school facility of St. Peter Lutheran Church during construction of a more permanent building on 24 Mile Road. By 1978, a total of 525 students enrolled, and expansion was going to be necessary. Traditions of excellence in academic preparation and commitment to spiritual growth have been carried forth throughout the years by the men and women who have made up the teaching faculty of Lutheran High North. (Both, courtesy of the Lutheran High School Association.)

In the years prior to 1853, a few faithful Lutheran families emigrated from Waldenburg, Schleswig, Germany, and settled in Macomb. The first congregation for Immanuel Lutheran Church was, as far as can be determined, the Geschows, Liebigs, Rehs, Duckwitzes, and Beggerows. These early settlers organized in 1853. (Courtesy of the Mount Clemens Public Library collection.)

Services began in the Reh barn, on Romeo Plank Road a half-mile from 21 Mile Road. The first resident pastor came in 1855, when Pastor J. Rauschert took up the call. The front part of this frame building served as the pastor's residence, and in the back were the church and the school. Pastor Rauschert served the congregation until 1865. (Courtesy of the Immanuel Lutheran Church collection.)

As the congregation grew, it was evident that the church was becoming too small. The first brick church was built in 1866, standing in the same place as the present structure. A time came when there were signs of the beginnings of a new congregation as an outgrowth of Immanuel. In 1882–1883, a total of 19 members from Immanuel formed St. Peter Lutheran Church, which is presently at 24 Mile and Romeo Plank Roads. (Courtesy of the Immanuel Lutheran Church collection.)

This was the first school building Immanuel Lutheran built, during the tenure of Rev. J. Rauschert. On April 4, 1866, Michael Pump was installed as the first teacher of the school. The school and congregation continued to grow, and in 1877, the school was divided into a north school, at 24 Mile and Romeo Plank Roads, and a south school, at 21 Mile and Romeo Plank Roads. The school building on 24 Mile Road was sold to the new congregation of St. Peter Lutheran in 1887 for $5 to serve as the new church. (Courtesy of the Immanuel Lutheran Church collection.)

The congregation continued to grow, and once again, the sanctuary needed to enlarge. In 1910, the present church building was dedicated. In 1929, the first confirmation class in English was conducted; in 1930, the first English worship services were held. By 1960, the German services were discontinued. (Courtesy of the Mount Clemens Public Library History collection.)

This is a portrait of Rev. George A. Sebald (1878–1962), who served as pastor of Immanuel Lutheran Church in Macomb Township for over three decades. The portrait was published with the news feature "Rev. George A. Sebald, 73, Marks 50 Years in Ministry" in the *Daily Monitor-Leader* on July 18, 1952. (Courtesy of the Mount Clemens Public Library collection.)

Immanuel Lutheran Church and cemetery are pictured during the winter. Many early residents of this area found their final resting place in this cemetery. (Courtesy of the Immanuel Lutheran Church collection.)

The school continued to grow, and in June 1961, the new school building was dedicated. By 1980, the worshipping attendance on a weekend was almost 400 families. When Pastor Michael Lutz came to Immanuel, the congregation began to show dramatic growth in its worship attendance. As attendance increased, additional worship services were needed, and there was again a necessity to expand the church facility. (Both, courtesy of the Immanuel Lutheran Church collection.)

Immanuel Lutheran School is seen here around 1937. From left to right are (first row) Mary Tillman, Shirley Morthum, unidentified, Earl Stier, two unidentified persons, and Mr. Hoffmeyer (teacher); (second row) Dick Stier, Stanley Kleino, Frances Pretzer, unidentified, Kathleen Kleino, Ester Schroeder, Ruth Papist, and Dolores Meitz; (third row) Fred Kuechenmeister, Donald Kuechenmeister, Kenneth Pretzer, Marvin Meitz, Wallace Pretzer, Roy Mittelstadt, Marvin Blank, and unidentified; (fourth row) Pauline Harder, unidentified, Dorothy Kuechenmeister, unidentified, Frances Meitze, and Pearl Papist. (Courtesy of the Larry and Christine Pretzer collection.)

Immanuel Lutheran School's students in grades four through six are pictured here in 1956. For the young lads, it may have been "flannel day." (Courtesy of the Larry and Christine Pretzer collection.)

An unknown grade at Immanuel Lutheran School is pictured here. The photograph lists a postal address of Mount Clemens in the 1962–1963 school year. Below is Immanuel Lutheran School, Room 1, on March 14, 1965. No student names are available. (Both, courtesy of the Larry and Christine Pretzer collection.)

Immanuel Lutheran Cemetery is located on 21 Mile and Romeo Plank Roads, next to the church. Many early residents of this area are buried in the cemetery, such as the Aherns, Behms, Engelmans, Glefkes, Grossers, Klockows, Leyers, Luchtmans, Penziens, Rehs, Rewoldts, Schoofs, and Stiers. (Both, author's collection.)

St. Peter Lutheran's history began when its forefathers came from Germany to this country for a new start. They joined Immanuel Lutheran in Waldenburg, as the teachings were the same as they had known in Germany. (Courtesy of the St. Peter Lutheran Historical collection.)

The area north of Waldenburg was growing at a very fast rate, and the need for a branch school at Romeo Plank and 24 Mile Roads became apparent in 1877 because of the distance the children had to walk. A parcel of land was purchased for $2.50, and the first wooden school was built. (Courtesy of the St. Peter Lutheran Historical collection.)

In 1882, nineteen members received a release from Immanuel Lutheran and organized St. Peter Lutheran Church of Macomb. They purchased the schoolhouse from Immanuel for $5; it served as their first church. Plans began for a new white frame church that was dedicated on December 10, 1882. The church was warmed by two pot-bellied stoves. All the wood for the stoves was cut and donated by the farmers in early fall. (Courtesy of the St. Peter Lutheran Historical collection.)

In 1927, the schoolhouse was moved on rolling logs across Romeo Plank Road to where the cemetery is today to make room for the new parsonage to be built. At one point in time, the older members recalled the early days when everyone came to church on foot or by horse and buggy. They would tie their horses to one of the hitching posts or put them in the horse stalls built across the street. (Both, courtesy of the St. Peter Lutheran Church Historical collection.)

As the number of students increased, the original wood schoolhouse was replaced by a brick school complete with a multipurpose basement. The ground-breaking and building for this new school took place in 1961–1962. The farmers of the congregation volunteered a great deal of time and talent to build the school. This building served for 31 years as St. Peter Lutheran School. (Courtesy of the Lutheran High School Association.)

Soon, the hitching posts and horses made way for the cars that brought the parishioners to the church services. Pictured here is a celebration of the church remodeling sometime in 1911. The remodel included adding a pair of windows and a pastor's study, raising the foundation, moving the altar back 14 feet, and lastly, installing a new coal furnace. (Courtesy of the St. Peter Lutheran Historical collection.)

This is an exterior view of St. Peter Lutheran Church, located at the corner of 24 Mile and Romeo Plank Roads. The church was built in 1882 and was replaced by a new structure in 1973. (Courtesy of the Mount Clemens Public History collection.)

This photograph of St. Peter Lutheran School was taken in 1926. From left to right are (first row) Oscar Teise, ? Brandenburg, Robert Eschenburg, Fred Danker, Ralph Hirsack, Emil Eschenburg, John Kogelmann, and Bernard Sohia; (second row) Nelson Luchtman, Walter Alwardt, Albert Stade, Fred Eckert, Richard Kage, Martin Schramm, and William Kreger; (third row) Mable Harms, Martha Teise, Ida Teise, Marguerite Schoof, Hilda Wondero, Lenore Kreger, Hattie Hirsack, Esther Beyerlein, Helen Hirsack, Mable Wondero, and Milda Beyerlein; (fourth row) Ronelda Bolle, Dorothy Harms, Hilda Gesch, Esther Danker, Esther Kreger, Gertrude Eschenburg, and Louise Bock, and teacher Mr. Danker; (fifth row) William Danker, William Penzien, Howard Hirsack, Arnold Eschenburg, Joa Penzien, Earl Rachow, Carl Kreger, and Alfred Sopha. (Courtesy of the St. Peter Lutheran Historical collection.)

During 1957, the church's 75th year, the school and church facilities were becoming inadequate, so plans were made for its future. A 14-acre parcel of land was purchased on the northwest corner of Romeo Plank and 24 Mile Roads at the cost of $1,000 per acre. A building committee was formed to plan for future needs. When the church became 90 years old, the second phase of the building project began. Below is an aerial view of the St. Peter community. (Both, courtesy of the St. Peter Lutheran Historical collection.)

Pictured here is the St. Peter Lutheran Church Cemetery. After the original church was dedicated in 1882, the cemetery was also consecrated behind the church on the southeast corner of 24 Mile and Romeo Plank Roads. Some local residents who have found their resting places here are the Engelbrechts, Kregers, Luchtmans, Penziens, and Schoofs. (Both, courtesy of the St. Peter Lutheran Historical collection.)

The farmland where St. Isidore Catholic Church stands today had its start as a strawberry patch. The first cross was made by parishioner Arthur Lambert from timbers sawn from oak logs from parishioner Frank Van Thomme's farm. In 2007, St. Isidore Catholic Church celebrated 50 years in the Macomb Township community. (Courtesy of the St. Isidore Catholic Church collection.)

On Sunday, December 4, 1949, a group of interested Catholic families met in an upstairs room of Stade's Market, located in the Dopp Building on the corner of Romeo Plank and 22 Mile Roads, for the express purpose of establishing a new parish in Macomb Township. Temporary officers were Frank Van Thomme (president), Leo Hellebuyck (vice president), Marcella Hellebuyck (secretary), and Omer Devriendt (treasurer). (Courtesy of the St. Isidore Catholic Church collection.)

St. Lawrence Catholic Church remained the place to worship for a number of years while plans were put into effect to start a new Macomb Township parish. In 1952, Roy Wade offered to sell the eight acres needed on the northwest corner of Romeo Plank and 23 Mile Roads. It was decided that Joseph Klinghammer's garage was a suitable place to say Mass initially. The new parish was called St. Isidore, after the patron saint of farmers, because the area was mostly farmland. (Courtesy of the St. Isidore Catholic Church collection.)

In 1959, a committee was selected to work on a temporary church on the 23 Mile Road site. St. Lawrence donated a two-classroom school building, and since it was too large to move in one piece, it was cut in half and moved separately. Remodeling of the building was done by local contractor Marvin Blank, with the volunteered help of many parishioners. (Courtesy of the St. Isidore Catholic Church collection.)

In 1958, a hall, classrooms, and space for the nuns' quarters were very much needed, and a building fund drive was set in motion with community help. By August 12, 1959, registration for first through sixth grades was held. (Courtesy of the St. Isidore Catholic Church collection.)

In 1967–1968, when the need for a larger building for worship services arose, a simple rectangular structure was dedicated with two or more classrooms and an enlarged convent. This structure was considered a temporary church because of the growth potential of the area. The image below, dated 1962–1963, is of the St. Isidore School, with an address at that time of Mount Clemens. In this image is Fr. Walter Schweihoffer, but the students' names are unavailable. (Above, courtesy of the St. Isidore Catholic Church collection; below, courtesy of the Larry and Christine Pretzer collection.)

The population of the parish community kept increasing due to the housing boom that occurred in the late 1980s, with Macomb Township leading the state in house permits. The 1987 planning committee is, from left to right, (first row) Kathy Arkles, Delphine Kolpacki, Monajean Ruppert, Victoria Surman, and Marge Stickney; (second row) Ed Christoff, Ray Weingartz, Harry J. Surman, Tom Beshke, Norman Ruppert, Chuck Finn, and George Lini. Absent from the image are Fred Wisinski, Madonna LaVerge, and Philip Hargrave. Below is a 1988 artist's rendering of the new St. Isidore Church. (Both, courtesy of the St. Isidore Catholic Church collection.)

Above the entrance of the 1967 St. Isidore Church sat a bell used to call people to worship. The 24-inch-diameter, cast iron alloy bell was manufactured by the Charles Singleton Bell Company of Hillsboro, Ohio. It was operated by someone pulling on the attached rope. When the building was demolished as part of the 2002 renovation, the bell was removed and preserved. It now sits in a position of prominence in the circle across from the main entrance as a tribute to the dedicated people who founded St. Isidore Catholic Church. Below, by 2002, demolition began on the current building site, and by 2005, the parishioners saw that the efforts of the long construction period were over and that they would now be able to enjoy a beautifully renovated church, social hall, classrooms, storage facilities, meeting rooms, and office area. (Left, author's collection; below, courtesy of the Matt Kush collection.)

Five

Moving Forward in Macomb

In June 2019, the township purchased the Wade Nursery, on the east side of Romeo Plank Road north of 23 Mile Road. The property had been in the Wade family for around 100 years, and the sale ended 55 years of business there. Its location in the middle of the township makes it convenient for most of Macomb residents. (Author's collection.)

In the 1970s, a Mr. Wade bought the original town hall and moved it from its 23 Mile Road location to his property to use as a storage building. The original town hall, still standing on the Wade property, could possibly be used as the new home for the Macomb Township Historical Commission. It would feature a museum for historical artifacts and research material that has been collecting in the basement of the current town hall. In the surrounding area, more sports fields and a general maintenance area would help the parks and recreation department fill the void in that part of the township. (Both, author's collection.)

Waldenburg Park, located on the north side of 21 Mile Road just east of Romeo Plank Road, is a community park covering approximately 17 acres. Waldenburg Park opened in 2002 as the first developed park space in Macomb Township. The park offers many amenities and is a great place for families to be active and enjoy the outdoors. The land was originally owned by the Webber family. (Both, author's collection.)

Macomb Corners Park is a 95-acre (35 developed) park site on the north side of 25 Mile Road just east of Luchtman Road. The park hosts sporting events and is an inviting location for family activities. The Macomb Township Parks and Recreation Department uses Macomb Corners Park as the host site for several community events throughout the summer. (Both, author's collection.)

The 15-acre Town Center Park, on the south side of 25 Mile Road just west of Broughton Road, is set up for the soccer enthusiast and functions as a small sports complex with four football fields. Below is an artist's rendering of the proposed Whitney Park in the Macomb Township Parks and Recreation Department's plan, to be located on the northeast corner of 24 Mile and Foss Roads, with a partial opening in 2021. (Right, author's collection; below, courtesy of the Macomb Township Parks and Recreation Department.)

The Westside Suburban School, which got its start in 1974, is the sixth ice hockey facility of a group around the Detroit metropolitan area. It opened at 54755 Broughton Road in Macomb Township in 2005 as Suburban Ice Macomb. It offers an ice-skating rink, hockey arena, and sports and fitness instruction—everything the ice enthusiast is looking for. (Courtesy of Suburban Ice Macomb and author's collection.)

Seen here is an artist's rendering of the new Clinton Macomb Public Library, North Branch, presently in the process of being built and opening in the fall of 2021. (Courtesy of the Clinton Macomb Public Library, North Branch collection, and Quinn Evans Architects.)

The Macomb Township Town Hall is located at 54111 Broughton Road, off of 25 Mile Road in Macomb. It opened on November 11, 2002, and the Macomb public found not only the treasurer's office but also the building department, assessing department, clerk's office, finance department, and supervisor's office all in one location. (Author's collection.)

The Macomb Township Recreation Center is a 92,000-square-foot facility with a fitness center, two gymnasiums, three rooms for birthday parties, two aerobics rooms, an indoor playground, and two pools—one with a lazy river and hot tub. Classes are offered weekly for youth, teens, adults, and seniors. (Author's collection.)

These brochures, sent to homeowners for the grand opening of the new Macomb Township Recreation Center in July 2004, show all the fees for membership and the services the center offered. (Both, courtesy of the Peggy Accrado collection.)

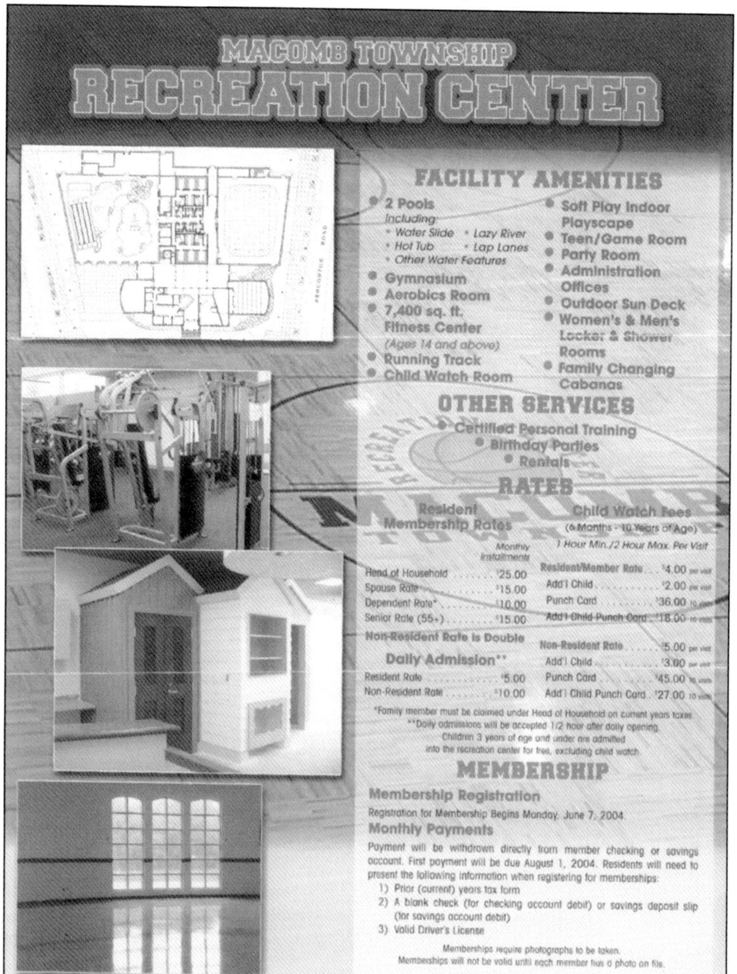

Bibliography

Echoes of Macomb: A Pictorial History of Our County. Mount Clemens, MI: *Macomb Daily*, 2001.

Eldredge, Robert F. *Past and Present of Macomb County, Michigan*. Chicago: Forgotten Books, 1905.

Leeson, Michael. *History of Macomb County*. Chicago: M.A. Leeson, 1882.

Naldrett, Alan. *Lost Towns of Eastern Michigan*. Charleston, SC: The History Press, 2015.

Remer, Deborah J. *If This Is Hastings, Then Where Is Hogs Hollow?: A Discovery of the Lost Villages in Oakland and Macomb Counties*. Rochester Hills, MI: Rochester Hills Museum at Van Hoosen Farm, 1990.

Through the Looking Glass: Macomb Township, 1920–1930. Mount Clemens, MI: *Macomb Daily*, 2000.

Consistent with our mission to preserve history on a local level, this book was printed in South Carolina on American-made paper and manufactured entirely in the United States. Products carrying the accredited Forest Stewardship Council (FSC) label are printed on 100 percent FSC-certified paper.

MADE IN THE USA